You Chose
To Be My Dad,
I Want to Hear
Your Story

A Guided Journal
For Stepfathers
To Share Their Life Story

Jeffrey Mason

Hear Your Story Books

"Life gave
me the gift
of you."

— Author Unknown

This Book
Holds & Shares
The Life Stories of:

_____

_____

"It's not
what we have
in life, but
who we have
in our life
that matters."

— Author Unknown

About This Book

They have many names and titles. Stepfather. Stepdad.Father. Dad. Bonus Parent.We often just refer to them by their first name.

Whatever we call them, we understand what they have brought to our lives.

We see their sacrifices. We remember the times they came when we needed help. We feel the many ways they show their love.

A step parent's love is unique because it is completely based on choice. They chose to us.

Their love for another person was so big and unconditional that it had enough room for an entire family with their histories, their traditions, their stories.

They then had to work the find right way to parent without being the parent. They couldn't just rely on rules and orders and discipline. Their way had to be one of listening, learning, supporting, and encouraging.

Little by little we found ourselves seeing them for who they are instead of who they are not. We saw their love and we felt their care and we found ourselves choosing them.

Just like they chose us. And because of that, all of us will never be the same.

IT'S YOUR BIRTHDAY!

"Fathering is not something perfect men do, but something that perfects the man." — Frank Pittman

What is your birthdate?

_____

What was your full name at birth?

_____

Were you named after a relative or someone else of significance?

_____

_____

_____

In what city were you born?

_____

What was your length and weight at birth?

_____

Were you born in a hospital? If not, where?

_____

_____

What were your first words?

_____

_____

IT'S YOUR BIRTHDAY!

"Any man can be a father, but it takes
someone special to be a dad." — Anne Geddes

How old were you when you started to walk?

_____

How old were your parents when you were born?

_____

_____

How did your parents describe you as a baby?

_____

_____

_____

_____

_____

_____

_____

_____

_____

_____

IT'S YOUR BIRTHDAY!

"We worry about what a child will become tomorrow,
yet we forget that he is someone today." — Stacia Tauscher

What stories have you been told about the day you were born?

_____

_____

_____

_____

_____

_____

_____

_____

_____

_____

_____

_____

_____

_____

IT'S YOUR BIRTHDAY!

"There are no perfect parents, but there are many
moments when being a parent is perfect." – Unknown

What is a favorite childhood memory of something you did
with family?

_____

_____

_____

_____

_____

_____

_____

_____

_____

_____

_____

_____

_____

WHAT HAPPENED
THE YEAR YOU WERE BORN?

"For the hand that rocks the cradle is the
hand that rules the world." — William Ross Wallace

Google the following for the year you were born:
What are some notable events that occurred?

_____

_____

_____

_____

What movie won the Academy Award for Best Picture?
Who won for Best Actor and Best Actress?

_____

_____

_____

What were a few popular movies that came out that year?

_____

_____

_____

_____

_____

WHAT HAPPENED THE YEAR YOU WERE BORN?

"The most important thing in the
world is family and love." — John Wooden

What song was on the top of the Billboard charts?

_____

Who was the leader of the country (President, Prime Minister, etc.)?

_____

What were a few popular television shows?

_____

_____

_____

_____

_____

What were the prices for the following items?
- A loaf of bread:
- A gallon of milk:
- A cup of coffee:
- A dozen eggs:
- The average cost of a new home:
- A first-class stamp:
- A new car:
- A gallon of gas:
- A movie ticket:

FAMILY TREE
"The ancestor of every action is a thought."
— Ralph Waldo Emmerson

My Great-Grandmother
(My Grandmother's Mom)

My Great-Grandmother
(My Grandfather's Mom)

My Great-Grandfather
(My Grandmother's Dad)

My Great-Grandfather
(My Grandfather's Dad)

My Grandmother
(My Mom's Mom)

My Grandfather
(My Mom's Dad)

My Mother

FAMILY TREE
"Each of us is tomorrow's ancestors."
— Unknown

_____
My Great-Grandmother
(My Grandmother's Mom)

_____
My Great-Grandmother
(My Grandfather's Mom)

_____
My Great-Grandfather
(My Grandmother's Dad)

_____
My Great-Grandfather
(My Grandfather's Dad)

_____
My Grandmother
(My Dad's Mom)

_____
My Grandfather
(My Dad's Dad)

_____
My Father

GROWING UP

"Even though you're growing up, you
should never stop having fun." — Nina Dobrev

How would you describe yourself when you were a kid?

_____

_____

_____

_____

Did you have a nickname when you were growing up? If
yes, how did you get it?

_____

Who were your best friends in your elementary school
days? Are you still in contact with them?

_____

_____

_____

_____

What were your regular chores? Did you get an allowance?
How much was it and what did you spend it on?

_____

_____

_____

GROWING UP

"It is easier for a father to have children than for
children to have a real father." — Pope John XXIII

Describe what your room looked like when you were
growing up. Was it messy or clean? Did you have paintings
or posters on the walls? What were the main colors?

_____

_____

_____

_____

_____

_____

_____

_____

What is one thing you miss about being a kid?

_____

_____

_____

_____

GROWING UP

"What can you do to promote world peace?
Go home and love your family." — Mother Teresa

Did you have braces when you were a kid?

_____

What are some of your favorite books from your early
childhood and/or teenage years?

_____

_____

_____

What was a typical Saturday like when you were a kid? What
did you spend the day doing?

_____

_____

_____

_____

_____

_____

_____

_____

GROWING UP

"Families are like branches on a tree. We grow in different directions, yet our roots remain as one." — Author Unknown

What is a favorite childhood memory of something you did with friends?

_____

_____

_____

_____

_____

_____

_____

_____

_____

_____

_____

_____

_____

TRIVIA

"The best inheritance a parent can give his children is a few
minutes of his time each day." — Orlando Aloysius Battista

What is your favorite flavor of ice cream?

_____

How do you like your coffee?

_____

_____

If you could live anywhere in the world for a year with all
expenses paid, where would you choose?

_____

_____

_____

How do you like your eggs cooked?

_____

Preference: cook or clean?

_____

What is your shoe size?

_____

What superpower would you choose for yourself?

_____

_____

TRIVIA

"There can be no keener revelation of a society's soul
than the way in which it treats its children." — Nelson Mandela

Do you have any allergies?

_____

_____

_____

What is your biggest fear?

_____

_____

What would you order as your last meal?

_____

_____

_____

_____

Have you ever broken a bone? Which one(s) and how?

_____

_____

What is your favorite flower or plant?

_____

THE TEENAGE YEARS

"Of all the titles I have been privileged to have,
'Dad' has always been the best." — Ken Norton

How would you describe yourself when you were a teenager?

_____

_____

_____

_____

How did you dress and style your hair during your teens?

_____

_____

_____

_____

_____

Did you hang out with a group or just a few close friends? Are you still close with any of them?

_____

_____

_____

THE TEENAGE YEARS

"Few things are more satisfying than seeing your
children have teenagers of their own." — Doug Larson

Describe a typical Friday or Saturday night during your
high school years.

_____

_____

_____

_____

Did you have a curfew?

_____

Did you date during your high school years?

_____

_____

Did you go to any school dances? What were they like?

_____

_____

_____

_____

Who taught you to drive and in what kind of car?

_____

_____

THE TEENAGE YEARS
"We never know the love of a parent till we
become parents ourselves." — Henry Ward Beecher

How old were you when you got your first car? What kind
of car was it (year, make, and model)?

_____

_____

What school activities or sports did you participate in?

_____

_____

_____

_____

_____

What did you like and dislike about high school?

_____

_____

_____

_____

_____

THE TEENAGE YEARS
"Having a teenager can cause parents to
wonder about each other's heredity." — Unknown

What were your grades like in high school?

_____

_____

Did you have a favorite subject and a least favorite?

_____

_____

_____

What are a few favorite songs from your high school years?

_____

_____

_____

_____

_____

_____

_____

_____

THE TEENAGE YEARS

"By the time a man realizes that maybe his father was right, he usually has a son who thinks he's wrong." — Charles Wadsworth

Knowing all you know now, what advice would you give to your teenage self? What might you have done differently in school if you knew then what you know now?

_____

_____

_____

_____

_____

_____

_____

_____

_____

_____

_____

_____

_____

THE TEENAGE YEARS

"Education is what remains after one has forgotten
what one learned in school." — Albert Einstein

Write about a teacher, coach, or other mentor who had a
significant impact on you when you were growing up.

_____

_____

_____

_____

_____

_____

_____

_____

_____

_____

_____

_____

_____

_____

BEGINNINGS
"We don't stop going to school when we graduate."
— Carol Burnett

What did you do after high school? Did you get a job, serve in the military, go to college or a trade school? Something else?

_____

_____

_____

_____

Why did you make this choice?

_____

_____

_____

_____

_____

If you went to college or trade school, what was your major/the focus of your education?

_____

_____

_____

BEGINNINGS
"it takes courage to grow up and become who you really are"
— ee cummings

How did this time period impact who you are today?

_____

_____

_____

_____

_____

If you could go back, what, if anything, would you change about this period of your life? Why?

_____

_____

_____

_____

_____

_____

_____

WORK & CAREER

"Even if you're on the right track, you'll get
run over if you just sit there." — Will Rogers

When you were a kid, what did you want to be when you grew up?

_____

_____

What was your first job? How old were you? How much were you paid?

_____

_____

How many jobs have you had during your lifetime? List a few of your favorites.

_____

_____

_____

_____

What is the least favorite job you have had?

_____

_____

_____

WORK & CAREER

"I'm a great believer in luck, and I find the
harder I work, the more I have of it." — Thomas Jefferson

Is there a job or profession your parents wanted you to
pursue? What was it?

_____

_____

_____

When people ask you what profession you are/were in, your
response is...

_____

_____

_____

How did you get into this career?

_____

_____

_____

_____

_____

_____

WORK & CAREER

"Choose a job you love and you will never
have to work a day in your life." — Confucius

What are/were the best parts of this profession?

_____

_____

_____

_____

_____

_____

_____

What aspects did you or do you dislike about it?

_____

_____

_____

_____

_____

_____

WORK & CAREER

"If people knew how hard I worked to get my mastery,
it wouldn't seem so wonderful after all." — Michelangelo

Who was the best boss you ever had? Why were they such
a good manager?

_____

_____

_____

_____

_____

What are some of your work and career-related
achievements that you are proudest of?

_____

_____

_____

_____

_____

_____

_____

TRIVIA

"Before I got married, I had six theories about raising children;
now, I have six children and no theories." — John Wilmot

Have you ever been told that you look like someone
famous? If yes, who?

_____

_____

_____

What is your morning routine?

_____

_____

_____

_____

What is a favorite guilty pleasure?

_____

_____

_____

Which television family most reminds you of your family?

_____

_____

TRIVIA

"Every father should remember that one day his child
will follow his example, not his advice." — Charles Kettering

Did you have braces? If yes, how old were you when you
got them?

_____

Do you like roller coasters?

_____

_____

What name would you choose if you had to change your
first name?

_____

Did you ever skip school?

_____

If yes, did you get away with it and what did you do
during the time you should have been in class?

_____

_____

_____

_____

_____

PARENTS & GRANDPARENTS
"Little children, headache; big children, heartache."
— Italian Proverb

Where was your mother born and where did she grow up?

_____

_____

_____

What three words would you use to describe her?

_____

_____

_____

In what ways are you most like your mother?

_____

_____

_____

_____

_____

_____

_____

PARENTS & GRANDPARENTS
"The soul is healed by being with children."
— Fyodor Dostoevsky

Where was your father born and where did he grow up?

_____

_____

_____

What three words would you use to describe him?

_____

_____

_____

In what ways are you most like your father?

_____

_____

_____

_____

_____

_____

_____

_____

PARENTS & GRANDPARENTS

"Pretty much all the honest truth telling there is in the
world is done by children." — Oliver Wendell Holmes

What is a favorite memory of your mother?

_____

_____

_____

_____

_____

_____

_____

_____

_____

_____

_____

_____

_____

PARENTS & GRANDPARENTS

"Pretty much all the honest truth telling there is in
the world is done by children." — Oliver Wendell Holmes

What is a favorite memory of your father?

_____

_____

_____

_____

_____

_____

_____

_____

_____

_____

_____

_____

_____

_____

PARENTS & GRANDPARENTS

"Study the past, if you would divine the future."
— Confucius

What is some of the best advice your mother gave you?

_____

_____

_____

_____

_____

_____

_____

_____

_____

_____

_____

_____

_____

_____

_____

PARENTS & GRANDPARENTS

"Grandmother — a wonderful mother with lots of practice."
— Author Unknown

What is some of the best advice your father gave you?

_____

_____

_____

_____

_____

_____

_____

_____

_____

_____

_____

_____

_____

PARENTS & GRANDPARENTS

"Parenthood remains the single greatest
preserve of the amateur." — Alvin Toffler

What was your mother's maiden name?

_____

Do you know from what part(s) of the world your
mother's family originates?

_____

_____

_____

Do you know your father's mother's maiden name?

_____

_____

Do you know from what part(s) of the world your father's
family originates?

_____

_____

_____

How did your parents meet?

_____

_____

_____

PARENTS & GRANDPARENTS
"Next to God, thy parents."
— William Penn

How would you describe their relationship?

_____

_____

_____

_____

_____

What were your parents' occupations?

_____

_____

_____

Did either of them have any unique talents or skills?

_____

_____

_____

Did either of them serve in the military?

_____

PARENTS & GRANDPARENTS

"There is no school equal to a decent home and no
teacher equal to a virtuous parent." — Mahatma Gandhi

What is a favorite family tradition that was passed down
from your parents or grandparents?

_____

_____

_____

What are a few of your favorite things that your mother
or father would cook for the family?

_____

_____

_____

_____

What were your grandparents like on your mother's side?

_____

_____

_____

_____

_____

_____

PARENTS & GRANDPARENTS
"A father's goodness is higher than the mountain,
a mother's goodness deeper than the sea." — Japanese Proverb

Do you know where your mother's parents were born and grew up?

_____

_____

_____

_____

What were your grandparents like on your father's side?

_____

_____

_____

_____

_____

Do you know where your father's parents were born and grew up?

_____

_____

_____

PARENTS & GRANDPARENTS

"A moment lasts for seconds but the memory of it lasts forever." — Unknown

Did you ever meet your great-grandparents on either side of your family? If yes, what were they like?

_____

_____

_____

_____

_____

_____

_____

_____

_____

_____

_____

_____

_____

PARENTS & GRANDPARENTS
"We don't remember days, we remember moments."
— Unknown

What other individuals had a major role in helping you grow up?

_____

_____

_____

_____

_____

_____

_____

_____

_____

_____

_____

_____

_____

YOUR SIBLINGS
"Brothers and sisters are as close as hands and feet."
— Vietnamese Saying

Are you an only child, or do you have siblings?

_____

Are you the oldest, middle, or youngest?

_____

List your siblings' names in order of their ages. Make sure to include yourself.

_____

_____

_____

_____

_____

Which of your siblings were you the closest with growing up?

_____

_____

Which of your siblings are you the closest with in your adult years?

_____

_____

YOUR SIBLINGS

"The greatest gift our parents ever gave us was each other."
— Author Unknown

How would you describe each of your siblings when they were kids?

_____

_____

_____

_____

_____

_____

How would you describe each of your siblings as adults?

_____

_____

_____

_____

_____

_____

_____

YOUR SIBLINGS

"First a brother, then a bother, now a friend."
— Author Unknown

In the following pages, share some favorite memories of each of your siblings. If you're an only child, feel free to share memories of close friends or cousins.

_____

_____

_____

_____

_____

_____

_____

_____

_____

_____

_____

_____

_____

YOUR SIBLINGS

"What causes sibling rivalry? Having more than one kid."
— Tim Allen

Memories...

_____

_____

_____

_____

_____

_____

_____

_____

_____

_____

_____

_____

_____

_____

YOUR SIBLINGS

"Siblings know how to push each other's buttons, but they also know how to mend things faster than anyone." — Unknown

Memories...

_____

_____

_____

_____

_____

_____

_____

_____

_____

_____

_____

_____

_____

YOUR SIBLINGS

"The advantage of growing up with siblings is that
you become very good at fractions." — Author Unknown

Memories...

_____

_____

_____

_____

_____

_____

_____

_____

_____

_____

_____

_____

_____

_____

_____

LET'S TALK ABOUT
BEING A STEPDAD

"It is easier to build strong children than
to repair broken men." — Frederick Douglass

When you were young, did you ever think you would be a father?

_____

What were your main concerns about becoming a stepparent?

_____

_____

_____

_____

_____

What excited you the most about it?

_____

_____

_____

_____

_____

LET'S TALK ABOUT
BEING A STEPDAD

"My father didn't tell me how to live. He lived and
let me watch him do it." — Clarence Budington Kelland

What five words describe how you want to be as a parent?

1. _____

2. _____

3. _____

4. _____

5. _____

What do you think are the biggest differences between
how kids are raised today and when you were young?

_____

_____

_____

_____

_____

_____

_____

_____

LET'S TALK ABOUT
BEING A STEPDAD

"Blessed indeed is the man who hears many
gentle voices call him father." — Lydia Maria Child

Knowing all you know now, what advice would you give
yourself when you first became a parent?

_____

_____

_____

_____

_____

_____

_____

_____

_____

_____

_____

LET'S TALK ABOUT
BEING A STEPDAD

"The father who does not teach his son his duties is
equally guilty with the son who neglects them." — Confucius

What are the best and hardest parts of being a stepdad?

_____

_____

_____

_____

_____

_____

_____

_____

_____

_____

_____

_____

_____

_____

WHEN YOU CHOSE US
"The older I get, the smarter my father seems to get."
— Tim Russert

How did you meet my mom?

_____

_____

_____

_____

What were your first impressions of her?

_____

_____

_____

_____

_____

When did you find out she had kids?

_____

_____

_____

_____

WHEN YOU CHOSE US

"Children are a poor man's riches."
— English Proverb

How did she describe each of his children to you?

_____

_____

_____

_____

_____

_____

_____

_____

_____

_____

_____

_____

_____

_____

WHEN YOU CHOSE US
"Adults are just outdated children."
— Dr. Seuss

What were your first impressions of each of us?

_____

_____

_____

_____

_____

_____

_____

_____

_____

_____

_____

_____

_____

WHEN YOU CHOSE US

"One father is more than a hundred schoolmasters."
— George Herbert

What did you and Mom do on your first date?

_____

_____

_____

_____

When did you know that you wanted to marry her?

_____

_____

_____

_____

What is your proposal story?

_____

_____

_____

_____

_____

_____

TRIVIA

"A father is a man who expects his children
to be as good as he meant to be." — Carol Coats

If you could do any one thing for a day, what would it be?

_____

_____

_____

What do you listen to when you are alone in the car?

_____

_____

How old were you when you got your first traffic ticket?
What was it for?

_____

_____

_____

Pick one that best describes you:
- ☐ I am very handy around the house.
- ☐ I can fix a few things.
- ☐ It is in everyone's best interest that I hire someone.

Do you or have you ever played a musical instrument?
Which one(s)?

_____

_____

TRIVIA

"Three things are always with me: my shadow,
my father's love, and his lessons." – Jeffrey Mason

What is your definition of success?

_____

_____

_____

What do you do better than anyone else in the family?

_____

_____

_____

If you could only eat three things for the next year (with
no effect on your health), what would you pick?

_____

_____

_____

What is a favorite memory from the last twelve months?

_____

_____

_____

_____

RELIGION & SPIRITUALITY

"Anyone who does anything to help a
child in his life is a hero." — Fred Rogers

What do you believe is the purpose of life?

_____

_____

_____

_____

_____

_____

_____

_____

_____

Which has the most impact on our lives: fate or free will?

_____

_____

_____

_____

_____

RELIGION & SPIRITUALITY

"A stepparent is so much more than a parent: they made
the choice to love when they didn't have to." —Unknown

Were your parents religious when you were growing up?
How did they express their spiritual beliefs?

_____

_____

_____

_____

_____

_____

_____

_____

_____

_____

_____

_____

_____

RELIGION & SPIRITUALITY

"A good father is one of the most unsung, unpraised, unnoticed,
and yet one of the most valuable assets in our society." — Billy Graham

If you are religious or spiritual, how have your beliefs and
practices changed over the course of your life?

_____

_____

_____

_____

_____

_____

_____

_____

_____

_____

_____

_____

_____

RELIGION & SPIRITUALITY

"Holding my child, I was turned from a boy into a guardian, a
provider, a helper, and a teacher. I had become a father." — Scott Jeffries

What religious or spiritual practices do you incorporate
into your daily life today, if any?

_____

_____

_____

_____

_____

_____

_____

Do you believe in miracles? Have you experienced one?

_____

_____

_____

_____

_____

_____

SPIRITUALITY & RELIGION

"Within you there is a stillness and a sanctuary to which
you can retreat at any time and be yourself." — Hermann Hesse

What do you do when times are challenging, and you need
to find additional inner strength?

_____

_____

_____

_____

_____

_____

_____

_____

_____

_____

_____

_____

_____

SPIRITUALITY & RELIGION

"Families are like branches on a tree. We grow in different
directions, yet our roots remain as one." — Author Unknown

Write about a time you found relief by forgiving someone.

_____

_____

_____

_____

_____

_____

_____

_____

_____

_____

_____

_____

_____

_____

_____

LOVE & ROMANCE

"We are asleep until we fall in love!"
— Leo Tolstoy, *War and Peace*

Do you believe in love at first sight?

_____

_____

_____

Do you believe in soulmates?

_____

_____

_____

How old were you when you had your first kiss?

_____

What age were you when you went on your first date?

_____

Can you remember who it was with and what you did?

_____

_____

_____

_____

_____

LOVE & ROMANCE
"The best thing to hold on to in life is each other."
— Audrey Hepburn

How old were you when you had your first steady relationship? Who was it with?

_____

How many times in your life have you been in love?

_____

_____

What are some of the most important qualities of a successful relationship?

_____

_____

_____

_____

_____

_____

_____

_____

_____

LOVE & ROMANCE
"Rejoice with your family in the beautiful land of life."
— Albert Einstein

Did you have any celebrity crushes when you were young?

_____

_____

_____

_____

Were you ever in a relationship with someone your parents did not approve of?

_____

_____

_____

Have you ever written someone or had someone write you a love poem or song?

_____

If yes, write a few lines that you may remember.

_____

_____

_____

_____

_____

LOVE & ROMANCE
"If I know what love is, it is because of you!"
— Hermann Hesse

In what ways do you feel your parents' relationship influenced how you have approached love and marriage?

_____

_____

_____

_____

_____

Write about a favorite romantic moment.

_____

_____

_____

_____

_____

_____

_____

TRAVEL

"Once a year, go someplace you've never been before."
— Dali Lama

Do you have a valid passport?

_____

How do you feel about cruises?

_____

_____

How do you feel about flying?

_____

What are a few of your favorite places that you've traveled to?

_____

_____

_____

_____

_____

_____

_____

_____

TRAVEL
"Life is short, and the world is wide."
— Author Unknown

What is a favorite travel memory?

_____

_____

_____

_____

_____

_____

_____

_____

_____

_____

_____

_____

_____

_____

_____

TRAVEL BUCKET LIST

"A ship in harbor is safe, but that is not what ships are built for."
— John A. Shedd

List the top 10 places you would visit if money and time were no concern.

1. _____

_____

2. _____

_____

3. _____

_____

4. _____

_____

5. _____

_____

TRAVEL BUCKET LIST

"People don't take trips, trips take people."
— John Steinbeck

6. _____

_____

7. _____

_____

8. _____

_____

9. _____

_____

10. _____

_____

TRIVIA

"Everything will be alright does not mean
everything will stay the same." — Unknown

What would you title your autobiography?

_____

_____

Do you think you could still pass the written portion of
the driver's test without studying?

_____

What is your favorite color?

_____

What is your favorite quote?

_____

_____

_____

Do you believe in life on other planets?

_____

If you could travel through time and had to choose, who
would you meet: your ancestors or your descendants?

_____

_____

_____

TRIVIA

"Life is a shipwreck, but we must not
forget to sing in the lifeboats." — Voltaire

What personal accomplishments are you most proud of?

_____

_____

_____

_____

_____

_____

What are five things you are grateful for?

_____

_____

_____

_____

If you were forced to sing karaoke, what song would you
perform?

_____

_____

_____

I HAVE...

"Life is a great big canvas, and you should
throw all the paint on it you can." — Danny Kaye

I have...

☐ Gotten a speeding ticket.

☐ Gotten out of a speeding ticket.

☐ Crashed a party.

☐ Been selected for a jury.

☐ Given someone a fake name or phone number.

☐ Been in a band.

☐ Had a near death experience.

☐ Performed CPR or the Heimlich Maneuver on someone.

☐ Driven in a country where they drive on the other side of the road.

☐ Been on a safari.

☐ Visited the Grand Canyon.

☐ Seen a meteor shower.

☐ Crowd-surfed at a music concert.

☐ Been to the Grand Canyon.

☐ Learned a second language.

☐ Been stuck in an elevator.

☐ Made a wish in the Trevi Fountain in Italy.

I HAVE...

"Fill your life with experiences. Not things. Have
stories to tell, not stuff to show." — Author Unknown

I have...

☐ Had my palm read.

☐ Had braces.

☐ Traveled to Greece.

☐ Gone ice skating.

☐ Gone snow skiing.

☐ Been to a tropical island.

☐ Ridden in a train.

☐ Grown a vegetable garden.

☐ Started a business.

☐ Experienced an earthquake.

☐ Been in a hurricane.

☐ Made a snow angel.

☐ Been where a tornado struck down.

☐ Lived in a foreign country.

☐ Slept outside under the stars.

☐ Gone sailing.

☐ Been to a rodeo.

☐ Gone deep sea fishing.

I HAVE...

"The greatest gifts you can give your children are the roots of responsibility and the wings of independence." — Denis Waitley

I have...

☐ Driven a tractor.

☐ Been in the middle of a mosh pit.

☐ Ridden in a horse-drawn carriage.

☐ Ridden a mechanical bull.

☐ Been a passenger in a private jet.

☐ Dyed my hair.

☐ Had my picture taken with someone famous.

☐ Ridden in a gondola in Venice.

☐ Been a maid of honor/best man.

☐ Re-gifted a gift.

☐ Been on television.

☐ Seen a UFO.

☐ Been knocked unconscious.

☐ Participated in a political protest.

☐ Attended the ballet.

☐ Adopted a pet.

☐ Witnessed the changing of the Guard in London.

☐ Attended the opera.

WHERE HAVE YOU LIVED?

"Fill your life with experiences. Not things. Have
stories to tell, not stuff to show." — Author Unknown

List the cities where you have lived during your lifetime.
Include the dates if you can remember them?

_____

_____

_____

_____

_____

_____

_____

_____

_____

_____

_____

_____

_____

SPORTS MEMORIES

"Anyone can be a father, but it takes
someone special to be a dad." — Wade Boggs

When you were a kid, did you ever think about being a
professional athlete? In which sports?

_____

_____

Growing up, what was your favorite sport? Did you have a
favorite team?

_____

_____

_____

_____

Who is your favorite player of all time in any sport?

_____

_____

_____

If money and time were no object, what sporting event
would you most want to attend?

_____

_____

_____

SPORTS MEMORIES

"My father gave me the greatest gift anyone could
give another person, he believed in me." — Jim Valvano

What was the first professional sporting event you attended
in person?

_____

_____

_____

What was the most crushing defeat you experienced playing
or watching a sporting event?

_____

_____

_____

Is there a sporting event you saw as a kid that you still
vividly remember?

_____

_____

_____

What is your favorite sports movie?

_____

_____

_____

POLITICAL STUFF
"What you teach your children, you also teach their children."
— Author Unknown

Which best describes how you feel about having political discussions:
- ☐ I would rather not.
- ☐ I prefer to have them with people whose views match mine.
- ☐ I love a good debate.

How old were you the first time you voted?

_____

What are the biggest differences in your political views today and when you were in your early twenties?

_____

_____

_____

_____

Have you ever taken part in a march or boycott? What issues, if any, could motivate you to join one?

_____

_____

_____

_____

POLITICAL STUFF

"In politics stupidity is not a handicap."
— Napoleon Bonaparte

When was the last time you voted?

_____

In what ways do you agree and disagree with the political choices of your children's generation?

_____

_____

_____

_____

_____

_____

If you woke up to find yourself in charge of the country, what are the first three things you would enact or change?

One: _____

_____

Two: _____

_____

Three: _____

_____

MOVIES, MUSIC, TELEVISION, & BOOKS

"If you want a happy ending, that depends, of course, on where you stop your story." — Orson Welles

What movie have you watched the greatest number of times?

_____

_____

What movie or television show can you remember loving when you were a kid?

_____

_____

Who would you cast to play yourself in the movie of your life? How about for the rest of your family?

_____

_____

_____

_____

_____

_____

_____

_____

MOVIES, MUSIC, TELEVISION, & BOOKS

"When I was a kid, my parents moved a lot,
but I always found them." — Rodney Dangerfield

What are your favorite genres of music?

_____

_____

_____

_____

Which decades had the best music?

_____

_____

_____

_____

What is the first record (or cassette, cd, etc.) you can remember buying or being given as a gift?

_____

_____

What song do you like today that would make your younger self cringe?

_____

_____

MOVIES, MUSIC, TELEVISION, & BOOKS

"Children are the living messages we send
to a time we will not see." — Neil Postman

What is a song from your teens that reminds you of a
special event or moment?

_____

_____

_____

What song would you pick as the theme song of your life?

_____

_____

_____

What was the first concert you attended? Where was it
held and when?

_____

_____

How has your taste in music changed over the years?

_____

_____

_____

_____

MOVIES, MUSIC, TELEVISION, & BOOKS

"Fatherhood is the best thing that could happen to me,
and I'm just glad I can share my voice." — Dwyane Wade

What television show from the past do you wish was still on the air?

_____

If you could be cast in any television show or movie, past or present, which one would you choose?

_____

What are some favorite books from your childhood and/or teenage years?

_____

_____

_____

What book or books have majorly impacted the way you think, work, or live your life?

_____

_____

_____

_____

_____

TOP TEN MOVIES
"Children need models rather than critics."
— Joseph Joubert

List up to ten of your most favorite movies:

1. _____

2. _____

3. _____

4. _____

5. _____

6. _____

7. _____

8. _____

9. _____

10. _____

TOP TEN SONGS

"The music is not in the notes, but in the silence in between."
— Wolfgang Amadeus Mozart

List up to ten of your most favorite songs:

1. _____

2. _____

3. _____

4. _____

5. _____

6. _____

7. _____

8. _____

9. _____

10. _____

TRIVIA
"It is not flesh and blood, but heart which
makes us fathers and sons." — Friedrich von Schiller

What is your favorite holiday and why?

_____

_____

_____

_____

Is there anything in your family's medical history that
your kids should know about?

_____

_____

_____

_____

_____

Which ten-year period of your life has been your favorite
so far and why?

_____

_____

_____

_____

TRIVIA

"Each day of our lives we make deposits in
the memory banks of our children." —Charles R. Swindoll

Who would you invite if you could have dinner with any
five people who have ever lived?

_____

_____

_____

_____

_____

What are some of your most favorite books?

_____

_____

_____

_____

_____

_____

_____

_____

_____

ROOM FOR MORE

"A tree's strength is found in its roots; its gifts, in its branches."
— Author Unknown

The following pages are for you to expand on some of your answers, to share more memories, and/or to write notes to your loved ones:

_____

_____

_____

_____

_____

_____

_____

_____

_____

_____

_____

_____

ROOM FOR MORE
"Be less curious about people and more curious about ideas."
— Marie Curie

_____

_____

_____

_____

_____

_____

_____

_____

_____

_____

_____

_____

_____

ROOM FOR MORE

"Let me love you a little more before you're not little anymore."
— Author Unknown

_____

_____

_____

_____

_____

_____

_____

_____

_____

_____

_____

_____

_____

_____

ROOM FOR MORE

"Of all the things my hands have held, the best, by far, is you."
— Unknown

_____

_____

_____

_____

_____

_____

_____

_____

_____

_____

_____

_____

_____

ROOM FOR MORE

"My Father's Day gift to you is letting you pretend to
be in charge of the family for a day." — Author Unknown

_____

_____

_____

_____

_____

_____

_____

_____

_____

_____

_____

_____

_____

ROOM FOR MORE

"A father isn't an anchor to hold us or a sail to carry us but a guiding light whose love shows us the way." — Author Unknown

_____

_____

_____

_____

_____

_____

_____

_____

_____

_____

_____

_____

_____

_____

ROOM FOR MORE

"The greatest gifts you can give your children are the roots of responsibility and the wings of independence." — Denis Waitley

_____

_____

_____

_____

_____

_____

_____

_____

_____

_____

_____

_____

_____

ROOM FOR MORE

"You will never look back on life and think,
'I spent too much time with my kids.'" — Author Unknown

_____

_____

_____

_____

_____

_____

_____

_____

_____

_____

_____

_____

_____

_____

HEAR YOUR STORY BOOKS

At **Hear Your Story**, we have created a line of books focused on giving each of us a place to tell the unique story of who we are, where we have been, and where we are going.

Sharing and hearing the stories of the people in our lives creates a closeness and understanding, ultimately strengthening our bonds.

Available at Amazon, all bookstores, and HearYourStoryBooks.com

- Mom, I Want to Hear Your Story: A Mother's Guided Journal to Share Her Life & Her Love

- Dad, I Want to Hear Your Story: A Father's Guided Journal to Share His Life & His Love

- Grandfather, I Want to Hear Your Story: A Grandfather's Guided Journal to Share His Life and His Love

- Tell Your Life Story: The Write Your Own Autobiography Guided Journal

- Life Gave Me You; I Want to Hear Your Story: A Guided Journal for Stepmothers to Share Their Life Story

- You Choose to Be My Dad; I Want to Hear Your Story: A Guided Journal for Stepdads to Share Their Life Story

HEAR YOUR STORY BOOKS

- To My Wonderful Aunt, I Want to Hear Your Story: A Guided Journal to Share Her Life and Her Love

- To My Uncle, I Want to Hear Your Story: A Guided Journal to Share His Life and His Love

- Mom, I Want to Learn Your Recipes: A Keepsake Memory Book to Gather and Preserve Your Favorite Family Recipes

- Dad, I Want to Learn Your Recipes: A Keepsake Memory Book to Gather and Preserve Your Favorite Family Recipes

- Grandmother, I Want to Learn Your Recipes: A Keepsake Memory Book to Gather and Preserve Your Favorite Family Recipes

- Grandfather, I Want to Learn Your Recipes: A Keepsake Memory Book to Gather and Preserve Your Favorite Family Recipes

- Aunt, I Want to Learn Your Recipes: A Keepsake Memory Book to Gather and Preserve Your Favorite Family Recipes

- Uncle, I Want to Learn Your Recipes: A Keepsake Memory Book to Gather and Preserve Your Favorite Family Recipes

- To My Girlfriend, I Want to Hear Your Story

- To My Boyfriend, I Want to Hear Your Story

- Mom & Me: Let's Learn Together Journal for Kids

ABOUT THE AUTHOR

Jeffrey Mason is the creator and author of the best-selling **Hear Your Story®** line of books and is the founder of the company **Hear Your Story®**.

In response to his own father's fight with Alzheimer's, Jeffrey wrote his first two books, **Mom, I Want to Hear Your Story** and **Dad, I Want to Hear Your Story** in 2019. Since then, he has written and designed over 30 books, been published in four languages, and sold over 300,000 copies worldwide.

Jeffrey is dedicated to spreading the mission that the little things are the big things and that each of us has an incredible life story that needs to be shared and celebrated. He continues to create books that he hopes will guide people to reflect on and share their full life experience, while creating opportunities for talking, listening, learning, and understanding.

Hear Your Story® can be visited at **hearyourstorybooks.com** and Jeffrey can be contacted for questions, comments, podcasting, speaking engagements, or just a hello at **jeffrey.mason@hearyourstory.com**.

He would be grateful if you would help people find his books by leaving a review on Amazon. Your feedback helps him get better at this thing he loves.

VIEW THIS BOOK
ON YOUR COMPUTER

We invite you to also check out HearYourStory.com, where you can answer the questions in this book using your smart phone, tablet, or computer.

Answering the questions online at HearYourStory.com allows you to write as much as you want, to save your responses and revisit and revise them whenever you wish, and to print as many copies as you need for you and your whole family.

Please note there is a small one-time charge to cover the cost of maintaining the site.

ISBN: 9798652765293

Made in the USA
Las Vegas, NV
01 June 2024